Barbados Sun Travel Guide

Fascinating History, What You Need to Know Before Traveling to Barbados, Hidden Gems, Tourist Attractions, Cuisine, Transportation and Security tips.
Errol S. Allen

Copyright

Table of Content

Chapter..2

1: Fascinating History of Barbados 2

Chapter 2: What you Need to know Before Traveling......................2
 to Barbados...2
Chapter 3 : Traveling to Barbados on Budget 2
Chapter 4 : Finding the Hidden Gems in Barbados.........................2
Chapter 5 : Locating Sightseeing Wonders in Barbados...................2
Chapter 6: Cuisine in Barbados 2
Chapter 7: Accommodation..2
Chapter 8: Transportation 2
Chapter 9: Safety tips : Do's and Don'ts 2
Chapter 10: Samples of Travel Itinerary 2
Introduction 1

- Barbados Culture and Tourism
- Barbados Govt and laws
- Barbados people and culture

- Pre - Travel tips for Barbados
- Basic Tourist Laws in Barbados
- Barbados Booking sites
- Good parking ideas and how not to dress like like a Tourist
- Barbados Weather and Travel Times

- Tips On How To Travel To Barbados on Budget
- Budget Friendly Activities In Barbados
- Barbados Travel Budget Options

- Hidden Gems in Barbados
- Unique Activities in Barbados
- Tourist Attractions in Barbados

- Sight seeing Wonders in Barbados
- Barbados Landmarks and Mountains
- Scenic Barbados Routes

- Barbados Food and drinks
- Barbados Local Delights
- Barbados Food and Drink Guide
- Barbados Eateries :Budget and Luxury
- Beer and Chocolate in Barbados

1

- Barbados Accommodation Options
- Pocket Friendly Accommodations In Barbados
- Children-Friendly Accommodation Options
- Barbados Car Rentals
- Barbados Boat Tours :Adult and Children

- Barbados Transportation Options
- Budget Friendly Transportation options
- Children-Friendly Transportation Options
- Barbados Car Rentals
- Barbados Boat Tours : Adult and Children

- Barbados Safety Tips
- Barbados Avoidance Guide Pocket Friendly Accommodations In Barbados
- Children-Friendly Accommodation in Barbados

- Samples 3 Days Itinerary
- Samples of 5 Days Itinerary
- Samples of 7 Days Itinerary
- Samples of 10 Days Itinerary

Introduction

Barbados

Barbados is a Caribbean island nation located in the North Atlantic Ocean, situated to the east of the Caribbean Sea. It covers an area of around 432 square kilometers (167 square miles) and has a population of approximately 287,000 people. Bridgetown, its capital and largest city, is a cultural and economic hub.

With a history shaped by indigenous peoples, colonization, and the transatlantic slave trade, Barbados gained independence from British rule on November 30, 1966, becoming a constitutional monarchy with a parliamentary democracy. The country maintains ties to the

British monarchy, with the monarch as the ceremonial head of state and a Governor-General representing the monarch locally. Barbados has a diverse economy that relies on tourism, international business, and offshore financial services. Its stunning beaches, warm climate, and vibrant culture make it a popular destination for travelers. The island is known for its distinctive coral-based landscape, with white sandy beaches surrounded by turquoise waters.

The culture of Barbados is a rich blend of African, European, and indigenous influences. Its music, including calypso, reggae, and soca, is an integral part of the local identity. Cricket is the most popular sport and holds a special place in the hearts of Barbadians. The country has made strides in education and healthcare, boasting one of the highest literacy rates in the Western Hemisphere. Barbados is also committed to environmental sustainability and has taken steps to protect its natural resources and marine ecosystems.

Overall, Barbados is a small but vibrant nation with a unique history, diverse culture, and picturesque landscapes that attract visitors from around the world.

Chapter 1: Fascinating History of Barbados

Barbados Culture & Tourism

Barbados is a vibrant Caribbean island known for its rich culture and beautiful tourism offerings. The island has a diverse history influenced by indigenous people, European colonization, and African heritage. Its culture is a blend of music, dance, art, and cuisine. The annual Crop Over Festival is a major cultural event featuring music, parades, and traditional arts.

Tourism is a significant part of Barbados' economy. Visitors are attracted to its stunning beaches, clear waters, and water sports. The historic Bridgetown and its Garrison are UNESCO World Heritage Sites. Visitors can explore plantation houses, botanical gardens, and enjoy local cuisine, including flying fish and cou-cou. The island's warm climate and friendly atmosphere make it a popular destination for relaxation and exploration.

Bajans and Bajan English

Barbados is an island nation located in the Caribbean region. The people of Barbados are known as Barbadians or Bajans. The population is ethnically diverse, with African, European, and East Indian ancestries being the most prominent. The African heritage stems from the historical period of slavery when Barbados was a major center of the transatlantic slave trade.

The official language of Barbados is English, which is spoken by the majority of the population. Bajan English, also known as Barbadian English, is a unique variation of English spoken by the locals. It includes elements of African languages, West African Pidgin English, and influences from other Caribbean dialects. Bajan English might be challenging for outsiders to understand due to its distinct vocabulary, pronunciation, and grammar.

The people of Barbados are known for their warmth, hospitality, and vibrant cultural expressions. The island's culture is a fusion of African, British, and Caribbean influences. The music genres of calypso, reggae, and soca are an integral part of the cultural scene. The Crop Over festival, held annually, is a lively celebration of Barbadian culture, featuring music, dance, and colorful costumes.

In recent times, Barbados has gained attention for its notable figures in various fields, such as the world-renowned singer Rihanna. The island's rich history, diverse population, and linguistic nuances make Barbados a fascinating place with a unique blend of influences.

Barbados Govt & Laws

Barbados is a parliamentary democracy with a constitutional monarchy, meaning the country recognizes the British monarch as its ceremonial head of state. The government consists of three branches: the executive, legislative, and judicial branches. The executive branch is headed by the Prime Minister, who is the head of government, and the Cabinet. The Prime Minister is responsible for running the government, making policy decisions, and representing Barbados on the international stage.

The legislative branch is composed of the bicameral Parliament, consisting of the House of Assembly and the Senate. The House of Assembly is made up of elected members who represent constituencies, while the Senate is composed of appointed members, including individuals recommended by the Prime Minister, the Leader of the Opposition, and other sources.

Barbados has its legal system based on English common law. The country's legal framework includes statutes, case law, and the Constitution. The legal system ensures the protection of fundamental rights and freedoms for Barbadian citizens. The judiciary is independent and consists of various courts, with the highest court being the Caribbean Court of Justice (CCJ) as the final court of appeal.

Laws in Barbados cover a wide range of areas, including civil, criminal, family, and commercial matters. The country has also taken steps to modernize its laws and adapt to changing societal needs.

It's important to note that my knowledge is based on information available up until September 2021, and there may have been developments or changes in Barbados' government and laws since that time.

Chapter 2: What you Need to know Before Traveling to Barbados

Barbados Pre-Travel Tips

Here are some pre-travel tips for your trip to Barbados:

1.Check Travel Requirements: Ensure you have a valid passport and check if you need a visa to enter Barbados based on your nationality. Also, review any

COVID-19 related travel restrictions or requirements.

2.Book Accommodation Early: Barbados is a popular destination, so it's advisable to book your accommodation well in advance to get the best options and prices.

3. Pack Accordingly: Pack lightweight, breathable clothing, swimsuits, sunscreen, sunglasses, and a hat. Don't forget insect repellent, comfortable walking shoes, and any medications you might need.

4. Travel Insurance: Purchase comprehensive travel insurance that covers medical expenses, trip cancellations, and any unexpected emergencies.

5. Health Precautions: Consult your doctor for any necessary vaccinations and health advice before traveling to Barbados. Carry a small medical kit with essentials like pain relievers, antacids, and band-aids.

6.Currency and Banking: The currency in Barbados is the Barbadian Dollar (BBD). Inform your bank about your travel dates so your credit/debit cards aren't flagged for suspicious activity.

7.Local Customs and Etiquette: Research local customs and etiquette to show respect for the culture. For example, wearing beach attire is acceptable at the beach, but it's advisable to cover up when you're away from the shoreline.

8.Language: English is the official language, so communication won't be an issue.

9.Electrical Outlets: Barbados uses electrical outlets with a voltage of 115V. You might need a plug adapter if your devices have a different type of plug.

10 Emergency Information: Save the contact information for your country's embassy or consulate in Barbados, as well as local emergency numbers.

11.Research Activities: Look into the various activities and attractions Barbados has to offer, such as visiting historical sites, enjoying water sports, and exploring local markets. Plan your itinerary accordingly.

13. Local Cuisine: Explore the local food scene and try Bajan specialties. Make note of any dietary restrictions or allergies you have.

14.Climate: Barbados has a tropical climate, so be prepared for warm and humid conditions. Check the weather forecast before you travel.

15.Photocopies of Documents: Make photocopies or digital scans of important documents like your passport, visa, travel insurance, and itinerary. Store them separately from the originals.

17. Stay Informed: Keep up-to-date with any travel advisories or local news related to Barbados before and during your trip.

Remember, planning ahead will help ensure a smooth and enjoyable vacation in Barbados!

Barbados Tourist Laws

This section of this guide will provide you with some general information about basic tourist laws in Barbados. Please note that laws and regulations can change, so it's a good idea to verify this information with up-to-date sources before your trip.

1.Entry Requirements: Visitors to Barbados typically need a valid passport and may also require a visa, depending on their nationality. It's important to check the visa requirements specific to your country before traveling.

2.Customs and Import Regulations: Travelers should be aware of the customs regulations regarding the import and export of goods. There are restrictions on bringing certain items into the country, such as firearms, illegal drugs, and some agricultural products. Make sure to declare any items of value when entering the country.

3.Local Laws and Regulations: Tourists are expected to adhere to local laws and regulations. This includes obeying traffic laws, not engaging in illegal activities, and respecting local customs and traditions.

4.Alcohol and Smoking: The legal drinking age in Barbados is 18. Smoking is banned in enclosed public spaces, including restaurants, bars, and public transportation.

5. Drugs: Possession, use, or trafficking of illegal drugs is strictly prohibited and can result in severe penalties, including imprisonment.

6.Beaches and Marine Life: Barbados has many beautiful beaches and coral reefs. It's important to respect the environment by not littering, damaging coral, or interfering with marine life.

7.Dress Code: While Barbados is a popular tourist destination, it's recommended to dress modestly when visiting religious sites or more conservative areas.

8.Health and Safety: Tourists should have comprehensive travel insurance that covers medical emergencies. It's also advisable to drink bottled or purified water to avoid health issues.

9.Driving: If you plan to rent a vehicle and drive in Barbados, remember that they drive on the left side of the road. You'll need to have a valid international driving permit or a local driving permit, which can be obtained from car rental agencies or the Barbados Licensing Authority.

10.Respect for Locals: Being courteous and respectful to locals is important. Engaging in rude or offensive behavior can lead to a negative experience during your stay.

Laws and regulations can change, and this information might not be up-to-date. I recommend checking with official Barbados government sources or your country's embassy or consulate for the latest information on tourist laws and regulations before your trip.

Barbados Booking Options

Barbados, a picturesque Caribbean island known for its stunning beaches and vibrant culture, offers a variety of booking sites to help you plan your trip. These websites allow you to book accommodations, flights, activities, and more. Here are a few notable booking sites for Barbados:

Expedia: Expedia is a popular online travel agency that offers a wide range of options for flights, hotels, car rentals, and vacation packages to Barbados. The platform allows you to customize your trip according to your preferences and budget.

Booking.com: This platform provides an extensive list of hotels, villas, and apartments in Barbados. You can filter your search based on various criteria such as price range, amenities, and guest reviews. The site also offers flexible booking options and often has special deals.

Airbnb: For those seeking unique accommodations, Airbnb offers a variety of options, including private rooms, entire homes, and even luxury villas in Barbados. This platform allows you to connect directly with hosts and experience local living.

TripAdvisor: Known for its comprehensive reviews and traveler ratings, TripAdvisor offers insights from fellow travelers about accommodations, restaurants, and attractions in Barbados. It's a great resource to help you make informed decisions.

Hotels.com: Similar to Booking.com, Hotels.com provides a range of hotel options in Barbados with user-friendly search and booking tools. The site often features discounts and rewards for frequent travelers.

CheapOair: If you're looking for competitive prices on flights to

Barbados, CheapOair is worth exploring. The platform offers a variety of flight options and allows you to compare prices from different airlines.

Barbados.org: This official tourism website for Barbados provides a wealth of information about the island's attractions, accommodations, events, and activities. It's a valuable resource to plan your trip and find direct links to various booking options.

JetBlue Vacations: If you're coming from the United States, JetBlue Vacations often offers package deals that include flights and accommodations in Barbados. It's a convenient way to book your entire trip at once.

Remember to compare prices across multiple platforms and read reviews from previous travelers to ensure you're making the best choices for your Barbados vacation. It's also a good idea to book well in advance, especially during peak travel seasons, to secure the best deals and availability.

Parking and Dress Tips

Here are some good parking ideas:

1.Resort Parking: Many hotels and resorts in Barbados offer free parking for their guests. If you're staying at one, take advantage of this convenience.

2.Public Lots: Look for public parking lots near popular attractions and beaches. They might have a daily fee, but it's often a convenient option.

3.Street Parking: Be sure to follow local parking regulations and signs if you're parking on the street. Avoid obstructing traffic or parking in no-parking zones.

4.Park and Ride: Some areas offer park-and-ride services, where you can park in a designated lot and take a shuttle to your destination. This can save you the hassle of finding parking in busy areas.

5.Early Bird Advantage: If you're planning to visit popular spots, arrive early to secure a parking spot before the crowds arrive.

6.Ride-Sharing: Consider using ride-sharing services instead of driving, especially if you're heading to a crowded area where parking might be limited.

As for dressing like a tourist in Barbados:

Casual Beachwear: Opt for lightweight and comfortable clothing suitable for the tropical climate. Avoid overly formal outfits.

Footwear: Choose comfortable sandals or breathable shoes. Leave heavy hiking boots at home unless you're planning intense outdoor activities.

Sun Protection: Don't forget to wear a hat, sunglasses, and apply sunscreen to protect yourself from the strong Caribbean sun.

Respect Local Culture: Barbados has a more conservative dress code in certain areas like towns and villages. Avoid overly revealing or offensive clothing.

Swimwear Etiquette: Reserve swimwear for the beach or pool. Wearing it outside these areas is generally considered inappropriate.

Bug Protection: Long sleeves and pants can help protect against mosquito bites during the evenings.

Evening Attire: For dining at upscale restaurants or attending events, pack some smart-casual outfits.

Respectful Attire: If you plan to visit religious or cultural sites, be sure to dress modestly out of respect.

Remember, blending in with the local style can enhance your experience while traveling and show respect for the culture you're visiting.

Barbados Weather and Travel Time

Barbados has a tropical climate with generally warm and pleasant weather year-round. The best time to visit is during the dry season, which typically spans from December to April. This period offers sunny days, low humidity, and comfortable temperatures ranging from the mid-70s to mid-80s Fahrenheit (24-30°C). However, keep in mind that this is also the peak tourist season, so accommodations might be pricier.

The rainy season runs from June to November, with the possibility of hurricanes from August to October. While prices are generally lower during this period, the weather can be more unpredictable, with higher humidity and occasional heavy rainfall.

If you're looking for a balance between good weather and fewer crowds, consider visiting Barbados in the shoulder seasons of May and November. These months offer decent weather and fewer tourists, making it a nice compromise between the peak and rainy seasons.

Chapter 3 : Traveling to

Barbados on Budget

Budget Tips for Barbados

Traveling to Barbados on a budget requires careful planning and smart decisions. Here are some tips to help you make the most of your trip without breaking the bank:

1.**Off-Peak Travel:** Consider traveling during the off-peak seasons (typically May-June and September-October) when accommodations and flights are more affordable.

2.**Flight Deals:** Look out for flight deals and compare prices across different airlines.

Flexibility with your travel dates can help you find cheaper options.

3.Accommodation: Opt for budget-friendly accommodations like guesthouses, hostels, or vacation rentals instead of luxury resorts. Booking in advance and using platforms like Airbnb can often yield good deals.

4.Local Cuisine: Enjoy local street food and dine at local eateries to save on food expenses. Sampling Barbadian specialties can be a memorable experience without overspending.

5.Public Transport: Utilize public buses and shared vans (ZR vans) to get around the island. They're more economical compared to taxis.

6.Free and Low-Cost Activities: Barbados offers stunning beaches, nature trails, and historic sites that don't cost a thing. Engage in free or low-cost activities like snorkeling, exploring botanical gardens, and attending local festivals.

7.Travel Insurance: While it may seem counterintuitive, having travel insurance can save you money in case of unexpected events, such as flight cancellations or medical emergencies.

8.Currency Exchange: Be mindful of currency exchange rates. Use local currency where possible to avoid unfavorable conversion rates and fees.

9.Avoid Peak Tourist Traps: Skip expensive tourist attractions that can eat into your budget. Instead, focus on the natural beauty and local experiences Barbados has to offer.

10.Pack Smart: Pack essential items like sunscreen, insect repellent, and reusable water bottles to avoid last-minute purchases that can add up.

11.Stay Connected Wisely: Use Wi-Fi in your accommodation or public spaces to avoid excessive data charges while staying connected.

12.Prepaid Travel Cards: Consider using prepaid travel cards to manage your spending and avoid high credit card fees.

Negotiate: Don't be afraid to negotiate prices, especially in markets or with vendors offering services.

13.Plan Ahead: Research and plan your activities in advance to avoid making impulsive and expensive decisions on the spot.

Traveling on a budget doesn't mean sacrificing experiences. By being resourceful and making thoughtful choices, you can have a fantastic time in Barbados without overspending.

Barbados Budget Activities

There are some some budget-friendly activities you can enjoy in Barbados and they include the following :

Beach Relaxation: Barbados is known for its stunning beaches. Spend a day soaking up the sun, swimming, and taking in the beautiful views without spending a dime.

Hiking: Explore the island's natural beauty by hiking through places like Welchman Hall Gully or Farley Hill National Park. It's a great way to experience the lush landscapes.

Farmers' Markets: Visit local farmers' markets like Cheapside Market in Bridgetown to sample fresh fruits, vegetables, and local products.

Oistins Fish Fry: On Friday nights, head to Oistins for an authentic Bajan experience. You can enjoy delicious seafood, music, and a lively atmosphere.

Garrison Savannah Racetrack: If you're visiting on a Saturday, you can watch horse racing at the Garrison Savannah Racetrack for a small entrance fee.

Animal Flower Cave: Explore the unique Animal Flower Cave, a natural cave with pools that you can swim in. Admission fees are reasonable.

Bridgetown Walking Tour: Take a self-guided walking tour of Bridgetown to discover its historic sites and architecture.

Barbados Museum & Historical Society: Learn about the island's history and culture at the Barbados Museum. Entrance fees are usually quite affordable.

Bathsheba: Enjoy the scenic beauty of Bathsheba, known for its dramatic coastal landscapes and unique rock formations.

Sunbury Plantation House: Immerse yourself in Barbadian

history by visiting Sunbury Plantation House, which offers guided tours showcasing the island's heritage.

While these activities are budget-friendly, it's always a good idea to check for any updated pricing or availability before you go.

Barbados Budget Travel options

Barbados offers a range of travel budget options to suit different preferences and financial considerations. Here are a few:

Affordable Accommodation: Look for guesthouses, hostels, or budget hotels to save on accommodation costs. These options might not have all the luxurious amenities, but they provide a comfortable stay at a lower price.

Local Cuisine: Enjoying local food at small eateries or street stalls can be much cheaper than dining at high-end restaurants. Barbadian cuisine offers a variety of delicious options that won't break the bank.

Public Transportation: Utilize buses and shared vans, known as "ZR vans," for cost-effective transportation around the island.

Taxis can be pricier, so reserve them for special occasions.

Free and Low-Cost Activities: Barbados boasts stunning beaches and natural beauty that can be enjoyed for free. Explore hiking trails, relax on the sand, or visit historical sites without spending much.

Happy Hour and Specials: Many bars and restaurants offer happy hour discounts or daily specials on drinks and meals. Take advantage of these to enjoy the island's nightlife without overspending.

Local Markets: Shop for souvenirs and essentials at local markets or street stalls for authentic items at better prices compared to touristy shops.

Group Activities: Participate in group tours or activities to share costs. This could include snorkeling, island tours, or water sports.

Avoid Peak Seasons: Travel during the shoulder season to get better deals on flights and accommodations. Peak seasons tend to be more expensive.

Plan Ahead: Research and plan your activities and meals in advance to avoid spontaneous overspending.

Limit Luxury Spending: While luxury experiences are available, keeping them to a minimum will help you stick to your budget.

Remember that even on a budget, you can have a wonderful time exploring Barbados and experiencing its culture, cuisine, and beautiful landscapes.

Chapter 4 : Finding the Hidden Gems in Barbados

Hidden Gems in Barbados

Barbados is known for its stunning beaches and vibrant culture, but it also holds some hidden gems that might not be as well-known to tourists. Here are a few:

1.Andromeda Botanic Gardens: Tucked away on the east coast, this peaceful garden showcases a diverse collection of tropical plants and flowers. It's a serene escape from the hustle and bustle, offering breathtaking coastal views.

2.Animal Flower Cave: This unique sea cave on the northern tip of the island features natural rock pools and formations, and is named after the "animal flowers" (sea anemones) that inhabit its pools. The views of the rugged coastline from here are truly mesmerizing.

3.Hunte's Gardens: Created by horticulturist Anthony Hunte, this enchanting garden is nestled in a sinkhole-like gully and offers an explosion of colors, plants, and meandering paths, making it a haven for nature lovers.

4.Bathsheba: Known for its dramatic rock formations, tidal pools, and powerful surf, Bathsheba is a paradise for surfers and photographers. The unique landscape provides a distinct contrast to the island's more serene beaches.

5.St. Nicholas Abbey: This historic plantation house is one of the last remaining Jacobean-style mansions in the Western Hemisphere. Visitors can explore the beautifully preserved architecture, gardens, and even a rum distillery on the grounds.

6.Cherry Tree Hill: A picturesque drive takes you to Cherry Tree Hill, where you'll find panoramic views of the island's lush landscapes and coastline. The location is particularly captivating during sunrise and sunset.

7.Fisherpond Great House: This lesser-known plantation house offers a glimpse into Barbados' colonial history. It's set on expansive grounds and showcases a blend of European and Caribbean architecture.

8.Welchman Hall Gully: This tropical ravine is a natural wonder filled with a variety of plant species, including rare and exotic trees. Guided tours provide insights into the area's flora and fauna.

9.Morgan Lewis Windmill: This well-preserved, historic windmill is one of the only two intact sugar windmills in the Caribbean. It's a testament to the island's sugar production heritage and offers fascinating insights into its past.

10.Gun Hill Signal Station: This former military signal station provides panoramic views of the island and features a collection of military memorabilia. It's a lesser-visited spot that offers both historical and scenic value.

These hidden gems in Barbados offer unique experiences beyond the typical tourist attractions, providing a deeper understanding of the island's natural beauty, history, and culture.

Barbados Unique Activities

Barbados offers a variety of unique activities that showcase its vibrant culture, stunning natural beauty, and rich history. Here are some details about some of these activities:

1.Crop Over Festival: This traditional festival celebrates the end of the sugarcane harvest with a series of lively events, including parades, concerts, calypso competitions, and elaborate costumes. The grand finale, called "Grand Kadooment," is a colorful street parade where participants dance through the streets in vibrant costumes.

2.Oistins Fish Fry: This is a must-do for seafood lovers. Oistins, a fishing town, comes alive every Friday night with a lively fish fry. Locals and visitors gather to enjoy fresh seafood, local dishes, and live music, creating a vibrant and social atmosphere.

3.Harrison's Cave: Explore the stunning underground world of Harrison's Cave. Take a guided tram tour through intricate limestone formations, crystal-clear pools, and flowing streams. It's an awe-inspiring experience to witness the natural beauty of the island's geology.

4.Swimming with Turtles: Barbados offers the unique opportunity to swim with sea turtles in their natural habitat. Numerous operators offer boat tours that take you to areas where you can snorkel alongside these graceful creatures, creating a memorable and educational experience.

5.Historical Bridgetown and its Garrison: A UNESCO World Heritage Site, this area features well-preserved colonial architecture and historic sites. Explore the George Washington House, which commemorates the visit of the future U.S. president, or visit the Barbados Museum and Historical Society to learn about the island's past.

6.Mount Gay Rum Distillery Tour: Barbados is famous for its rum, and the Mount Gay Rum Distillery offers an insightful tour into the island's rum-making history. Learn about the distillation process, the history of rum production, and of course, enjoy tastings of their world-renowned rum.

7.Atlantis Submarine Tour: Experience the underwater world of Barbados without getting wet. The Atlantis Submarine takes you on a unique underwater journey to explore coral reefs, marine life, and even shipwrecks, providing a different perspective of the island's coastal beauty.

8.Cricket Matches: Cricket is a passion in Barbados, and watching a local cricket match is a great way to immerse yourself in the island's sports culture. The Kensington Oval is a renowned venue where you can catch exciting matches and feel the energy of the crowd.

9.Explore Animal Flower Cave: Located at the northern tip of the island, the Animal Flower Cave is a natural cave system with stunning ocean views. The cave got its name from the sea anemones that resemble animals. It's a unique blend of geological wonder and coastal beauty.

10.Explore Bathsheba Beach: This rugged and picturesque beach on the east coast is famous for its massive rock formations, strong waves, and serene ambiance. It's a favorite spot for surfers, photographers, and those seeking a more off-the-beaten-path experience.

These activities represent just a glimpse of the unique experiences Barbados has to offer. Whether you're interested in history, culture, nature, or adventure, there's something for everyone on this beautiful Caribbean island.

Barbados Top Attractions

Barbados, a beautiful Caribbean island known for its stunning beaches, vibrant culture, and rich history, offers a plethora of tourist attractions. Here are some of the top attractions to explore:

1.Bridgetown: The capital city boasts historical sites like the Parliament Buildings, St. Michael's Cathedral, and the

Nidhe Israel Synagogue, the oldest synagogue in the Americas. The city also has shopping districts and a bustling harbor.

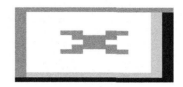

2.Harrison's Cave: This limestone cavern is a natural wonder, featuring stunning stalactites, stalagmites, and underground streams. Visitors can take guided tram tours through the cave to witness its breathtaking formations.

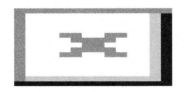

3.Bathsheba: This picturesque coastal village on the east coast is famous for its rugged beauty, with dramatic rock formations, powerful waves, and serene tide pools. It's a favorite spot for surfers and photographers.

4.Crane Beach: Known for its pink-tinged sand and striking turquoise waters, Crane Beach is a must-visit. The cliffside views and gentle waves make it perfect for swimming, sunbathing, and relaxing.

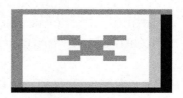

5.Animal Flower Cave: Located on the northern tip of the island, this cave offers stunning ocean views and a natural pool that's home to sea anemones, locally known as "animal flowers." It's a unique and serene spot.

6.St. Nicholas Abbey: This 17th-century plantation house offers a glimpse into Barbados' colonial history. Visitors can tour the beautifully preserved mansion, explore the gardens, and learn about the island's sugar production past.

7.Oistins Fish Fry: Every Friday night, the town of Oistins comes alive with a lively fish fry. It's a chance to savor delicious seafood, enjoy live music, and experience the island's vibrant social scene.

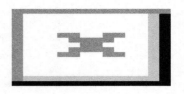

8.Andromeda Botanic Gardens: Nature enthusiasts will appreciate this lush tropical garden, home to a diverse collection of plant species from around the world. It's a peaceful oasis for a leisurely stroll.

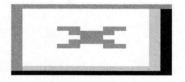

9.Mount Gay Rum Distillery: Barbados is known for its rum, and a visit to the Mount Gay Rum Distillery offers insights into the island's rum-making history. Guided tours take you through the process and offer tastings.

10. Barbados Wildlife Reserve:
This reserve allows you to observe animals like green monkeys, tortoises, and various bird species in a natural habitat. The monkeys, in particular, are a major draw.

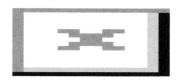

11. George Washington House:
A lesser-known historical gem, this house was where a young George Washington stayed during his only visit to Barbados. The museum offers insights into his time on the island.

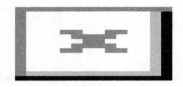

12.Farley Hill National Park:
This former plantation estate now serves as a park with lush gardens and the ruins of a mansion. The park offers great views and is a popular spot for picnics.

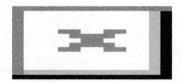

These attractions showcase the diverse offerings of Barbados, from its natural beauty to its rich history and culture.

Whether you're interested in exploring its caves, enjoying its beaches, or immersing yourself in its heritage, Barbados has something for every type of traveler.

Chapter 5 : Locating Sightseeing Wonders in Barbados

Barbados Landmarks & Vie

Barbados is a relatively flat and low-lying island in the Caribbean, which means it doesn't have traditional mountains like some other islands in the region. Instead, it features gently rolling hills and generally flat terrain. However, there are a few notable high points and landmarks on the island:

Mount Hillaby: Though not a towering peak, Mount Hillaby is the highest point on the island, reaching an elevation of around 336 meters (1,102 feet). It offers panoramic views of the surrounding landscape and the coastline.

Cherry Tree Hill: This is a picturesque spot along the eastern coast of Barbados, offering stunning vistas of the Atlantic Ocean and the lush countryside. It's more of a hilltop viewpoint than an actual mountain.

St. Nicholas Abbey: This historic plantation house is one of Barbados' landmarks. It's an architectural gem dating back to the 17th century and is surrounded by well-preserved gardens. Despite its name, it's not an abbey but a beautifully restored sugar plantation.

Harrison's Cave: While not a mountain, Harrison's Cave is a natural wonder. It's an intricate limestone cave system with stunning stalactites, stalagmites, and crystal-clear pools. Visitors can explore the cave on guided tram tours.

Barbados Wildlife Reserve: This reserve is home to a variety of animals, including green monkeys, deer, tortoises, and more. It's a great place to experience the island's natural beauty and observe its native wildlife.

St. John's Parish Church: This historic church is known for its stunning architecture and commanding hilltop position. It offers sweeping views of the coastline and surrounding countryside.

Bridgetown: While not a natural landmark, Bridgetown is the capital and largest city of Barbados. It's home to several historical sites, including St. Mary's Anglican Church, Parliament Buildings, and the historic Garrison area, a UNESCO World Heritage site.

Animal Flower Cave: Located at the northern tip of the island, this sea cave is named after the sea anemones found in its pools. It's both a geological wonder and a popular tourist attraction.

While Barbados might not have towering mountains, its unique blend of historical sites, natural wonders, and scenic viewpoints make it a captivating destination to explore.

Barbados Scenic Routes

Barbados offers a variety of scenic routes that showcase its natural beauty and cultural charm. One such route is the scenic drive along the east coast. This drive takes you through rugged cliffs, stunning vistas of the Atlantic Ocean, and quaint villages, such as Bathsheba known for its world-class surf breaks.

Another picturesque route is the West Coast Road, also known as the Platinum Coast. This drive offers breathtaking views of the Caribbean Sea, luxurious resorts, and upscale dining options. The calm waters and golden beaches are a sight to behold along this route.

Heading inland, the Scotland District route showcases the island's lush interior. You'll encounter rolling hills, sugar cane fields, and charming villages. The Andromeda Botanic Gardens along this route are a treat for nature enthusiasts.

For a historic and cultural journey, the Heritage Highway takes you through UNESCO-listed Bridgetown and its Garrison area. You'll pass historic buildings, museums, and landmarks that tell the story of Barbados' past.

Don't miss the Flower Forest route, leading you to the Hunte's Gardens. This route is a feast for the senses, with colorful flowers, exotic plants, and serene pathways that wind through a tropical paradise.

These routes collectively provide a diverse and captivating view of Barbados' landscapes, from its stunning coastlines to its lush interiors and historic sites. Whether you're interested in nature, history, or simply enjoying the picturesque views, Barbados has a route for every traveler to explore.

Barbados is known for its stunning natural landscapes and vibrant cultural scene. While it doesn't have traditional mountains like some other destinations, it offers picturesque highland areas with lush scenery and panoramic views. One such place is the Scotland District, located in the northeastern part of the island. This elevated region offers breathtaking vistas of the coastline and the Atlantic Ocean.

As for galleries, Barbados has a rich artistic community and a number of galleries that showcase both local and international talent. The Barbados Museum and Historical Society, located in the UNESCO-listed Garrison Historic Area, features a diverse collection of historical artifacts and artwork. The gallery often hosts exhibitions highlighting the island's history, culture, and contemporary art scene.

Another notable gallery is the Arlington House Museum in Speightstown. This interactive museum not only offers insights into the island's past but also showcases the works of local artists. The exhibits here provide a comprehensive understanding of Barbadian heritage and creativity.

Additionally, the ArtSplash Centre in Hastings is a hub for contemporary art, featuring a range of exhibitions and workshops. It's a great place to explore modern Barbados and Caribbean art.

While not traditional mountains, the island's elevated areas and galleries combine to offer visitors a unique blend of natural beauty and cultural enrichment in Barbados.

Chapter 6: Cuisine in Barbados

Bajan Food and Drinks

Barbadian cuisine, often referred to as Bajan cuisine, is a rich and diverse blend of flavors influenced by African, Indian, British, and Caribbean traditions. The island's tropical climate provides a wide range of ingredients that contribute to its vibrant food scene. Here's a closer look at some of the food and drink varieties you can find in Barbados:

Food:

Flying Fish and Cou-Cou: This is the national dish of Barbados. Flying fish, a staple in Bajan cuisine, is often paired with cou-cou, a cornmeal and okra-based dish similar to polenta. It's often accompanied by gravy or sauce.

Macaroni Pie: A popular side dish, macaroni pie is a Caribbean twist on macaroni and cheese. It's creamy and cheesy, often baked to perfection.

Pudding and Souse: Pudding typically refers to steamed sweet potato or breadfruit mixed with spices, while souse is pickled pork, usually served with onions, cucumbers, and hot peppers.

Fish Cakes: These are deep-fried dough balls filled with seasoned fish, often served as a popular snack or appetizer.

Bajan Black Cake: Similar to a traditional British fruitcake, this dense and rich dessert is made with fruits soaked in rum and is a must-have during festive occasions.

Conkies: Typically enjoyed around Independence Day, Conkies are sweet treats made from cornmeal, coconut, pumpkin, and spices, all wrapped in banana leaves and steamed.

Drinks:

Rum: Barbados is known as the birthplace of rum, so it's no surprise that the island boasts a wide variety of rum options. Brands like Mount Gay and Foursquare are renowned for their premium rums.

Mauby: This is a traditional Bajan drink made from the bark of the mauby tree, mixed with spices like clove and cinnamon. It has a unique flavor and is often enjoyed chilled.

Rum Punch: A classic Caribbean cocktail, Bajan rum punch typically includes rum, lime juice, sugar, water, and a sprinkle of nutmeg. The famous recipe is "One of Sour, Two of Sweet, Three of Strong, Four of Weak."

Sorrel: A popular festive drink, sorrel is made from hibiscus flowers infused with spices like cinnamon and cloves. It's often sweetened and served chilled.

Coconut Water: Fresh coconut water is a refreshing and hydrating choice, easily found at local vendors and markets across the island.

Banks Beer: This is the most famous local beer in Barbados, enjoyed by both locals and visitors. It's a light lager perfect for the island's climate.

Barbados' culinary scene offers a delightful array of flavors, reflecting its history and cultural influences. From hearty traditional dishes to refreshing tropical beverages, exploring Bajan food and drinks is a treat for the senses.

Barbados Local Delights

Barbados is known for its rich culinary heritage and local delights that reflect the island's cultural diversity. Here are some popular local dishes:

Flying Fish and Cou-Cou: This is the national dish of Barbados. Flying fish, which are abundant in the waters surrounding the island, are typically seasoned and pan-fried. Cou-Cou, a cornmeal-based side dish, is often served alongside. The cou-cou is similar to polenta and has okra mixed in for a unique texture.

Macaroni Pie: A beloved comfort food, macaroni pie is a baked dish made with macaroni pasta, cheese, eggs, and spices. It's often served at family gatherings and celebrations.

Pudding and Souse: This dish is a combination of pickled pork (souse) and a steamed sweet potato and cornmeal pudding. The pork is marinated in a tangy, spicy mixture, while the pudding provides a nice contrast with its sweetness.

Bajan Black Cake: This dessert is a Caribbean version of fruitcake. It's made with rum-soaked fruits, molasses, and spices like nutmeg and cinnamon. The cake is dark, dense, and full of flavor, often enjoyed during special occasions.

Fish Cutters: A popular street food, fish cutters are sandwiches made with fried fish fillets, often marinated in a tangy sauce. The fish is usually served in a salt bread roll and accompanied by lettuce, tomato, and sometimes cheese.

Bakes: These are deep-fried bread rolls, similar to doughnuts but less sweet. Bakes are commonly served with fried fish, cheese, or ham for a quick and satisfying meal.

Pepperpot: This hearty stew features meat (often pork), vegetables, and spices, simmered together to create a rich and flavorful dish. It's usually enjoyed with rice or bread.

Conkies: Conkies are sweet treats made from cornmeal, coconut, pumpkin, raisins, and spices like nutmeg and cinnamon. The mixture is wrapped in banana leaves and steamed until cooked.

Cassava Pone: A dessert made from grated cassava, this dish is sweetened with coconut, sugar, and spices, then baked to create a dense, chewy cake.

Rice and Peas: This dish combines rice, pigeon peas (or black-eyed peas), coconut milk, and various seasonings. It's a staple in Barbadian cuisine and often served alongside meat or fish dishes.

These local delights showcase the diverse flavors and influences that make up Barbadian cuisine. From seafood to traditional stews, sweet treats, and flavorful side dishes, Barbados offers a tantalizing culinary experience that reflects its history and culture.

Barbados Food & Drinks Guide

Here's a detailed guide to Barbadian food and drinks:

1. Flying Fish Cutter:

A signature Barbadian dish, the Flying Fish Cutter is a sandwich made with freshly fried flying fish, typically served on a salt bread roll along with lettuce, tomato, and sometimes a zesty Bajan hot sauce. It's a must-try when visiting Barbados.

2. Cou-Cou and Flying Fish:

This is a traditional Barbadian dish often referred to as the national dish. Cou-Cou is made from cornmeal and okra, creating a smooth and slightly sticky texture. It's usually paired with stewed or fried flying fish and a flavorful tomato-based sauce.

3. Fish and Seafood:

Given its coastal location, Barbados boasts an array of delicious seafood options. Along with flying fish, you'll find dishes like grilled marlin, mahi-mahi, lobster, and shrimp prepared in various ways.

4. Pudding and Souse:

Pudding and Souse is a beloved Saturday dish in Barbados. Pudding refers to a spiced sweet potato or bread-based sausage, while Souse consists of pickled pork (or sometimes other meats) served with onions, cucumbers, and spicy seasoning.

5. Macaroni Pie:

Similar to a baked macaroni and cheese casserole, Barbadian Macaroni Pie adds a local twist with the inclusion of seasonings like mustard, thyme, and occasionally minced meat. It's a comfort food staple.

6. Bajan Black Cake:

A dessert closely associated with Christmas celebrations, Bajan Black Cake is a rich, dense fruitcake soaked in rum. It's made with ingredients like raisins, currants, cherries, and prunes, all soaked in rum for weeks before baking.

7. Rum Punch:

Rum is an integral part of Barbadian culture, and Rum Punch is a popular drink that reflects this. Made with rum, sugar, lime juice, and a touch of nutmeg, it's refreshing and potent. The famous rhyme "One of sour, two of sweet, three of strong, and four of weak" refers to the key ingredients and proportions.

8. Banks Beer:

Banks Beer is the local brew and a favorite among locals and visitors alike. It's a light and crisp lager, perfect for enjoying on a sunny day by the beach.

9. Mauby:

A unique Bajan drink, Mauby is made from the bark of the mauby tree and infused with spices like cinnamon and clove. It has a distinct flavor that's both refreshing and slightly bitter.

10. Sea Egg:

A delicacy often enjoyed in Barbados, sea eggs are a type of sea urchin. They are typically served raw with a splash of lime juice, providing a briny and flavorful experience.

11. Jug Jug:

Another festive dish, Jug Jug is often associated with Christmas. It's made from pigeon peas, corned beef, and guinea corn flour, cooked together with herbs and spices to create a hearty stew-like dish.

Barbados offers a culinary journey that blends local flavors with international influences. Exploring the island's food and drink scene is an essential part of experiencing its vibrant culture and warm hospitality.

Budget Eateries in Barbados

Here are a few budget-friendly eateries in Barbados along with their addresses:

Cuzz's Fish Stand:

Address: Hwy 1, Bridgetown, Barbados

1. Enjoy freshly caught fish and seafood dishes at this local favorite by the beach.

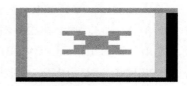

Oistins Fish Fry:
Address: Oistins, Christ Church, Barbados
2. This vibrant Friday night fish fry offers an array of affordable seafood options in a festive atmosphere.

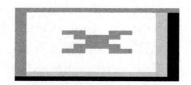

Peggy's Place:
Address: Bay St, Bridgetown, Barbados
A charming spot for traditional Bajan dishes at reasonable prices, including flying fish and cou-cou.

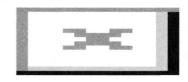

Brown Sugar Restaurant:

Address: Bay St, Bridgetown, Barbados

3. Sample a mix of Caribbean and Bajan flavors with their buffet-style lunch, offering value for money.

Cheapside Café:

Address: Cheapside Market, Cheapside, Bridgetown, Barbados

4. A local market where you can enjoy delicious Bajan food at budget-friendly prices.

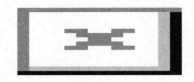

Just Grillin':

Address: Lanterns Mall, Hastings, Christ Church, Barbados

   5. A casual eatery known for its grilled dishes and affordable menu options.

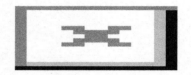

Café Moya:

Address: Lanterns Mall, Hastings, Christ Church, Barbados

   6. Grab a quick bite of sandwiches, wraps, and pastries without breaking the bank.

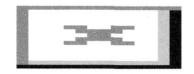

Bubba's Sports Bar:

Address: Rockley Main Rd, Christ Church, Barbados

7. A lively spot with pub-style food and affordable drinks, perfect for a casual meal.

Champers:

Address: Skeete's Hill, Christ Church, Barbados

8. While not the cheapest, Champers offers a more upscale experience with affordable lunch specials and a stunning ocean view.

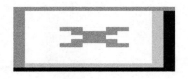

Roti Den:
Address: Brewster's Road, Christ
Church, Barbados

9. Savor authentic Indian and
   Caribbean flavors with
   their rotis and curry dishes
   at reasonable prices.

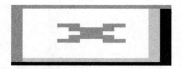

Remember to check the current
operating hours and availability,
as circumstances can change.
Enjoy your culinary adventures
in Barbados!

Barbados Luxury Eateries
Barbados offers a variety of
luxury eateries that provide
exquisite dining experiences.
Here are a few notable options
along with their addresses:
The Cliff Restaurant - Derricks,
St. James, Barbados

1. Known for its stunning oceanfront views and innovative cuisine, The Cliff offers a blend of Caribbean and international flavors.

Cin Cin By The Sea - Prospect, St. James, Barbados
2. This upscale restaurant boasts a contemporary Mediterranean menu and an elegant ambiance overlooking the Caribbean Sea.

The Tides Restaurant - Holetown, St. James, Barbados
3. Situated in a charming colonial-style building, The Tides is renowned for its fusion of Caribbean and international dishes.

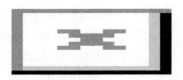

Daphne's - Paynes Bay, St. James, Barbados

4. With a focus on Italian cuisine, Daphne's offers beachfront dining and an extensive wine list.

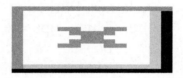

Champers Restaurant & Wine Bar - Skeetes Hill, Christ Church, Barbados

5. Set on a cliff overlooking the ocean, Champers is known for its seafood, international dishes, and extensive wine selection.

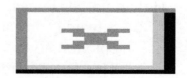

La Cabane - Prospect, St. James, Barbados

6. Offering beachfront dining, La Cabane is famous for its French-inspired cuisine and romantic atmosphere.

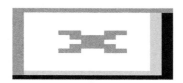

The Restaurant at South Sea - St. Lawrence Gap, Christ Church, Barbados

7. This restaurant provides a blend of Bajan and international flavors in an oceanfront setting.

Lone Star Restaurant - Mount Standfast, St. James, Barbados

8. Lone Star offers a fusion of Mediterranean and Caribbean cuisine with a chic beachfront vibe.

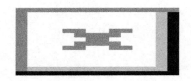

Nishi Restaurant - Prospect, St. James, Barbados

9. Known for its contemporary Japanese cuisine, Nishi offers an array of sushi and other Japanese delicacies.

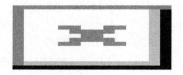

The Mews - Second Street, Holetown, St. James, Barbados

10. Situated in a charming courtyard, The Mews serves eclectic dishes in a cozy and intimate setting.

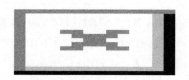

Remember to check for the latest information regarding addresses, menus, and reservations before visiting these luxury eateries. Enjoy your culinary journey in Barbados!

Barbados: Wine & Chocolate

Barbados, known for its stunning beaches and vibrant culture, also offers a delightful experience for wine and chocolate enthusiasts. While the island may not be as famous for its wine production as some other regions, it certainly offers a range of quality options to pair with its delectable chocolates.

When it comes to wine, Barbados boasts a growing wine culture with a selection that includes both international and local offerings. Many restaurants and bars on the island feature well-curated wine lists that cater to a variety of preferences.

Whether you're a fan of reds, whites, or rosés, you can find options that complement the tropical climate and cuisine. Chardonnay, Sauvignon Blanc, and even some sparkling wines can be enjoyed as refreshing choices in the warm Barbadian atmosphere.

Local wineries in Barbados are also making their mark. The unique terroir of the island contributes to the production of some delightful wines. One of the most well-known wineries is Saint Nicholas Abbey, which produces small batches of high-quality wines, including a range of aged rums. These local wines offer visitors a taste of the island's distinct flavors while celebrating its heritage.

Pairing wine with chocolates is a refined and delightful experience that allows you to explore the intricate flavors of both elements. The richness of dark chocolates often pairs well with red wines like Merlot or Cabernet Sauvignon, while white chocolates might be better suited to sweeter wines like Riesling or Moscato.

Experimenting with different combinations can lead to some surprising and delightful taste sensations.

Barbados' chocolate scene is equally captivating. The island's rich history and agriculture have contributed to the cultivation of cocoa. There are several chocolate producers and artisans on the island who craft exquisite chocolates from locally sourced cocoa beans. These chocolates often showcase unique flavors and textures that reflect the tropical environment, making them an ideal match for the island's wines.

Visitors to Barbados can enjoy guided tours of chocolate-making processes, exploring the journey from cocoa bean to the final product. Some of these tours include visits to cocoa plantations and demonstrations of chocolate-making techniques, offering a deeper understanding of the craft.

In recent years, Barbados has also seen the emergence of various events and festivals centered around wine and chocolate. These events provide locals and tourists with the opportunity to sample an array of wines, chocolates, and confections in a festive and convivial atmosphere. It's a chance to engage with the island's culinary and cultural offerings while expanding one's palate.

In conclusion, while Barbados might not be a traditional wine or chocolate powerhouse, it certainly offers a charming and unique experience for enthusiasts of both. From exploring local wineries to savoring handcrafted chocolates, the island's offerings cater to those seeking a delightful and refined culinary adventure amid its breathtaking landscapes.

Chapter 7: Accommodation

Barbados Accommodation Options

Barbados offers a diverse range of accommodation options to cater to various preferences and budgets. Here are some details about the types of accommodations you can find on the island:

Luxury Resorts and Hotels: Barbados is renowned for its upscale resorts and hotels. These establishments often offer stunning oceanfront views, private beaches, world-class amenities, and top-notch services. Some popular options include Sandy Lane, The Crane Resort, and Coral Reef Club.

Boutique Hotels: For a more intimate experience, boutique hotels are a great choice. These smaller, independently-owned properties often boast unique designs, personalized service, and a more local ambiance. Places like Little Arches Boutique Hotel and The Atlantis Hotel fall into this category.

All-Inclusive Resorts: Many resorts in Barbados offer all-inclusive packages, which can be convenient for travelers who want to have most of their expenses covered upfront. These packages typically include accommodations, meals, beverages, and some activities.

Vacation Rentals and Villas: Vacation rentals and private villas provide a home-away-from-home experience. They are ideal for families or larger groups, offering amenities like fully equipped kitchens, private pools, and spacious living areas. Websites like Airbnb and Vrbo list numerous options.

Guesthouses and Bed & Breakfasts: These options

provide a more authentic local experience. Guesthouses and B&Bs are often family-run and offer comfortable rooms, homemade breakfasts, and a chance to interact with locals.

Apartment Rentals: Apartments are a great option for travelers who prefer a bit more independence and the ability to cook their meals. Many apartments are conveniently located near beaches and attractions.

Hostels: While not as prevalent as in some other destinations, Barbados does have a few hostels that offer budget-friendly accommodations. These are often favored by backpackers and solo travelers.

Camping: For the adventurous, some camping sites are available, allowing you to stay close to nature. Keep in mind that camping options may be limited and require advance booking.

Eco-Lodges: If you're environmentally conscious, consider staying at an eco-lodge. These lodges are designed to minimize their impact on the environment and offer a sustainable lodging option.

Cruise Ships: Barbados is a popular cruise destination, and some travelers opt to stay on cruise ships that dock at the island. This can be an interesting way to experience Barbados alongside other Caribbean destinations.

When choosing your accommodation in Barbados, consider factors such as your budget, preferred location, desired amenities, and the type of experience you want to have. Keep in mind that prices and availability can vary based on the time of year and special events on the island.

Budget Accommodation in Barbados

There are a few budget-friendly accommodation options in Barbados and they include the following :

Dover Beach Hotel: Located at St. Lawrence Gap, Christ Church, this hotel offers affordable rates and is just steps away from the beautiful Dover Beach.

South Gap Hotel: Also situated in St. Lawrence Gap, this hotel offers oceanfront rooms and is close to restaurants and nightlife.

Rostrevor Hotel: Another option in St. Lawrence Gap, this hotel provides self-catering apartments with kitchenettes, making it convenient for budget-conscious travelers.

Pirates Inn: Found in the Hastings area, this hotel offers a mix of traditional and modern accommodations, and it's a short distance from the beach.

Coconut Court Beach Hotel: This hotel is located in Hastings, Christ Church, and offers affordable oceanfront rooms and easy access to a white sandy beach.

Melbourne Inn: Situated in Bridgetown, the capital city, this inn provides budget-friendly rooms and is close to various attractions.

Please note that addresses might change over time, so it's a good idea to search for the most up-to-date information online before making any reservations.

Luxury Accommodations in Barbados

Barbados offers a range of luxury accommodations for travelers seeking a lavish experience. Some renowned options include:

1.Sandy Lane: This iconic resort in St. James is known for its opulent suites, world-class golf courses, and pristine beachfront. Address: Sandy Lane, St. James, Barbados.

2.Cobblers Cove: Situated in Speightstown, this boutique hotel boasts elegant suites, a serene beach, and personalized service. Address: Road View, Speightstown, Barbados.

3.The Crane Resort: A historic resort in St. Philip, famous for its stunning cliffside views, private plunge pools, and exceptional spa. Address: Crane, St. Philip, Barbados.

4.Sandy Haven: A chic beachfront property in St. James, offering contemporary suites and easy access to the vibrant nightlife of Holetown. Address: Paynes Bay, St. James, Barbados.

5.Port Ferdinand: Located in Six Men's Bay, this luxury marina resort features lavish villas with private berths and access to upscale amenities. Address: Six Men's Bay, St. Peter, Barbados.

6.Coral Reef Club: A family-owned luxury resort in St. James, known for its lush gardens, elegant suites, and renowned spa. Address: Holetown, St. James, Barbados.

7.Sandy Cove: Situated in Derricks, this beachfront haven offers spacious penthouses and an intimate atmosphere. Address: Derricks, St. James, Barbados.

Royal Westmoreland: A prestigious golf and spa resort in St. James, featuring luxurious villas with stunning views of the **8.Caribbean Sea. Address**: St. James, Barbados.

These accommodations offer a blend of comfort, exclusivity, and scenic beauty, making your stay in Barbados truly unforgettable.

Children-Friendly Accommodation in Barbados

Certainly! Here are more details about some child-friendly accommodations in Barbados:

The Crane Resort: This luxurious resort offers spacious suites and villas with kitchen facilities, which can be convenient for families. It has a kids' club, playground, and a family-friendly pool area. The Crane Beach is known for its pink sand and gentle waves, making it suitable for children to enjoy.

Turtle Beach by Elegant Hotels: This all-inclusive resort provides family-friendly amenities such as a kids' club, water sports, and various dining options. The Flying Fish Kids' Club offers a range of supervised activities for children of different age groups. The resort's beachfront location also adds to the appeal for families.

Ocean Two Resort & Residences: This modern resort offers spacious suites and apartments with kitchenettes. It has a family-friendly pool and direct beach access. The resort's location in the St. Lawrence Gap area provides access to various dining and entertainment options suitable for families.

Crystal Cove by Elegant Hotels: Another all-inclusive option, Crystal Cove, provides a kids' club, water sports, and evening entertainment suitable for families. The calm waters at the resort's beach make it a safe and enjoyable place for children to swim and play.

Bougainvillea Barbados: This resort offers apartment-style accommodations with kitchen facilities, ideal for families. It has a kids' club and a range of activities such as water sports and tennis. The resort's location on the south coast allows easy access to nearby attractions.

Remember to inquire about the specific amenities, activities, and services offered by each resort to ensure they align with your family's preferences and needs.

Additionally, be sure to check recent reviews and verify the current status of the accommodations before making your reservation.

Chapter 8: Transportation

Barbados Transportation Options

Barbados offers a range of transportation options for both locals and visitors to explore the island. Here are the details about some of the transportation modes available:

Public Buses: Barbados has an extensive public bus system that covers most of the island's major routes. The buses are relatively affordable and provide a convenient way to travel between towns and attractions. The blue government-operated buses are known for their distinctive appearance and are a common sight on the roads.

ZRs and Minibuses: These are privately owned minibusses, often referred to as "ZRs" due to their distinctive license plate prefix. They offer a more informal and flexible mode of transportation, though they might have varying levels of comfort and adherence to schedules. ZRs are known for playing loud music and might pick up and drop off passengers anywhere along their route.

Taxis: Taxis are readily available in Barbados, and they can be hailed on the street or hired from designated taxi stands. They provide a more personalized and comfortable mode of transportation, especially for those who prefer convenience and privacy.

Car Rentals: Renting a car is a popular option for tourists who want to explore the island at their own pace. Several international car rental companies have offices in Barbados, offering a variety of vehicles for different budgets.

Bicycle Rentals: Some areas of Barbados, especially along the coast, are quite bike-friendly. Bicycle rental shops provide a means for eco-conscious travelers to explore the island while enjoying its natural beauty.

Scooter Rentals: Scooter and moped rentals are available in certain areas, offering a fun and efficient way to navigate through traffic and explore the island's attractions.

Walking: In some areas, such as along the coast or within towns, walking can be a pleasant and practical way to get around. Just keep in mind that Barbados has a tropical climate, so staying hydrated and protecting yourself from the sun is essential.

Ride-Sharing Apps: As of my last update in September 2021, ride-sharing services like Uber were not available in Barbados. However, it's worth checking if these services have become available since then.

Ferries and Catamarans: If you're interested in island hopping, there are ferry and catamaran services that connect Barbados to nearby islands like St. Lucia, St. Vincent, and Grenada.

Public Transportation Cards: Barbados also offers the Bajan Travel Smart Card, which can be used on public buses to facilitate cashless payments and provide discounts for frequent travelers.

It's important to note that traffic can be congested during peak hours in certain areas, so it's a good idea to plan your transportation accordingly. Always verify the most up-to-date information before making travel arrangements, as services and options might have evolved since my last update.

Barbados Transport Options

Barbados offers a variety of transportation options catering to both luxury and budget travelers. Luxury Transportation Options:

1.Private Car Services: Luxury travelers can opt for private car services, often provided by high-end hotels and resorts. These services offer personalized transfers in comfortable and stylish vehicles.

Limousines and Chauffeur Services: For a touch of elegance, limousines and chauffeur services are available for hire. They provide a luxurious and convenient way to explore the island.

Yacht Charters: Barbados is surrounded by crystal-clear waters, making yacht charters a popular choice for luxury transportation. Travelers can rent private yachts for a day of sailing and exploring the coastline.

Helicopter Tours: Helicopter tours offer a unique way to see the island from above. Companies provide aerial tours, often including stunning views of the coastline and landmarks.

Budget Transportation Options:

Public Buses: Barbados has an extensive public bus system that is affordable and well-connected. Buses are the primary mode of transportation for many locals and budget-conscious travelers. The buses cover most of the island's popular routes.

ZR Vans: ZR vans are privately operated minivans that offer an inexpensive way to get around. While they can be a bit crowded, they are a popular choice among locals and tourists alike.

Shared Taxis: Shared taxis, known as "route taxis," follow specific routes and can be a cost-effective option for short distances. Passengers share the ride with others heading in the same direction.

Rental Cars: While not the cheapest option, renting a car can provide flexibility and convenience for exploring the island. There are several rental companies to choose from, and rates vary based on the type of vehicle and duration of rental.

Biking and Walking: Barbados is relatively small and has some bike-friendly areas, making cycling and walking feasible for shorter distances. It's a great way to soak in the local atmosphere and enjoy the scenery.

Carpooling: Some local apps or platforms offer carpooling services, allowing travelers to share rides with others heading in the same direction, which can help reduce transportation costs.

Whether you're looking for a luxurious experience or trying to stick to a budget, Barbados offers a range of transportation options that cater to different preferences and needs.

Child-Friendly Transport Options

Children-friendly transportation options prioritize safety, comfort, and convenience for young passengers. Some popular choices include:

1.**School Buses**: These are specifically designed for transporting students, featuring safety measures such as seat belts, high seat backs, and flashing lights. They provide a consistent and supervised mode of transportation.

2.**Family Cars:** Vehicles with spacious interiors, proper child safety seats, and rear seat entertainment can make family trips enjoyable and safe.

3.Minivans: Minivans offer ample space for families, with sliding doors for easy access and versatile seating arrangements. Some models even come equipped with built-in entertainment systems.

4.SUVs: Certain SUV models offer third-row seating, accommodating larger families. They often have advanced safety features and enough room for strollers, sports equipment, and other essentials.

5.Public Buses: Many cities have child-friendly public bus services equipped with designated spaces for strollers and priority seating for families.

6.Trains: Trains are spacious and offer the opportunity for children to move around during longer journeys. Some trains have play areas or designated family compartments.

7.Subways and Trams: Many urban transit systems offer child-friendly services, such as spacious cars for strollers and designated family zones.

8.Bike Trailers and Cargo Bikes: For eco-conscious families, bike trailers and cargo bikes can be attached to bicycles, allowing parents to transport their children and groceries while promoting a healthy lifestyle.

9.Ride-Sharing Services: Some ride-sharing apps offer options for car seats and boosters, ensuring safe transportation for young passengers.

10.Walking and Biking: Short distances can be covered on foot or by bike, promoting exercise and quality time with children.

Remember, regardless of the transportation mode, ensuring child safety with appropriate car seats, seat belts, and proper restraint systems is crucial.

Car Rental Services

Barbados is a popular tourist destination, and there are several car rental services available on the island. Here are some details about car rental services and a few addresses you can consider:

Drive-A-Matic Car Rentals: One of the most well-known car rental companies in Barbados. They offer a wide range of vehicles, including sedans, SUVs, and minivans. Their main office is located at the Grantley Adams International Airport, Christ Church.

Stoutes Car Rental: A family-owned company that offers a variety of vehicles, including luxury cars and SUVs. They have a main office in Holetown, St. James, and a location at the Grantley Adams International Airport.

Courtesy Rent-A-Car: This company offers a diverse fleet of vehicles and provides airport pickup and drop-off services. They have multiple locations, including one at the Grantley Adams International Airport and another in Bridgetown, the capital city.

Top Class Car Rentals: They offer affordable rates and a range of vehicles. You can find them at the Grantley Adams International Airport and in Bridgetown.

Caribbean Rentals: Another reputable option with various vehicle choices. They have a location in Bridgetown and at the Grantley Adams International Airport.

Direct Car Rentals: Known for friendly service and a variety of vehicles. They are situated in

Christ Church, not far from the airport.

Executive Rentals: If you're looking for luxury and high-end cars, this company might be your choice. They are located at Christ Church and also provide airport services.

Don't forget that it's advisable to book your car rental in advance, especially during peak tourist seasons. When picking up your rental car, make sure you have a valid driver's license, a credit card, and any required documentation.

Boat Experiences in Barbados

Barbados offers wonderful boat experiences for both adults and children. For adults, you can enjoy catamaran cruises along the scenic coastline, with options to snorkel, swim with turtles, and indulge in delicious local cuisine and drinks. The Carlisle Bay Marine Park is a great spot for snorkeling and discovering vibrant marine life.

For children, the Atlantis Submarine Tour is an exciting option, providing an underwater adventure to explore reefs and shipwrecks without getting wet.

Pirate-themed cruises are also popular, featuring interactive activities, treasure hunts, and even mock battles on the high seas.

Both adults and children can enjoy glass-bottom boat tours, giving you a unique view of the underwater world. Additionally, a visit to the Barbados Wildlife Reserve and Grenade Hall Signal Station provides educational experiences that include learning about local wildlife and history.

Have it at the back of your mind to check the age restrictions and preferences of each tour to ensure everyone has a fantastic boat experience in Barbados.

Chapter 9: Safety tips : Do's and Don'ts

Here are some detailed security tips for staying safe in Barbados:

1. **Personal Belongings:**
   - Keep your valuables, such as passports, cash, and electronics, in a hotel safe or a secure place in your accommodation.

- Use a money belt or a hidden pouch to carry your important documents and cash when you're out.

2. **Public Spaces:**
   - Be cautious in crowded areas, as they can be targets for pickpocketing or petty theft.
   - Avoid displaying expensive items like jewelry or flashy electronics in public, as it can attract unwanted attention.

3. **Transportation:**
   - Use reputable and licensed taxi services. If you're using public transportation, keep an eye on your belongings.
   - If renting a car, lock your doors and keep windows up when driving. Don't leave valuables visible inside the car.

4. **Beach Safety:**

- While enjoying the beautiful beaches, don't leave your belongings unattended. Use waterproof bags to protect your valuables while swimming.
- Follow posted signs and lifeguard instructions. Some beaches might have strong currents or other hazards.

5. **Nightlife:**
   - Stick to well-known and busy areas if you're going out at night. Avoid poorly lit or deserted streets.
   - Travel in groups when possible, and never accept drinks from strangers.

6. **Scams and Fraud:**
   - Be cautious of unsolicited offers, especially those that seem too good to be true. Scammers might target tourists

with various schemes.

7. **Local Laws and Customs:**
   - Familiarize yourself with local laws and customs to avoid inadvertently offending or breaking any rules.
   - Drug possession and use are illegal and can lead to severe penalties.

8. **Health Precautions:**
   - Stay hydrated, especially in the tropical climate. Drink bottled or purified water and avoid tap water.
   - Apply sunscreen regularly to protect yourself from the strong Caribbean sun.

9. **Emergency Information:**
   - Keep a list of emergency contact numbers, including local police, medical services, and your

country's embassy or consulate.

10. **Stay Informed:**

- Keep an eye on local news and follow any travel advisories or updates provided by your government.

Remember, while Barbados is generally safe for tourists, taking these precautions can greatly enhance your safety and peace of mind during your visit.

Barcelona Crowds Avoidance

Barcelona is a popular tourist destination, but it can get crowded and overwhelming at times. Here are some tips to help you navigate the city while avoiding the crowds:

1. **Timing**: Visit popular attractions early in the morning or later in the afternoon to avoid peak crowds. Weekdays tend to be less busy than weekends.

2. **Off-Peak Season**: Consider visiting during the shoulder seasons (spring and fall) when the weather is still pleasant, but the crowds are thinner

compared to the peak summer months.

3. **Alternative Attractions**: Explore lesser-known attractions and neighborhoods that are equally charming but attract fewer visitors. Examples include Gràcia, Poblenou, and El Raval.

4. **Park Güell**: This iconic park can get very crowded. To avoid the crowds, buy your ticket in advance and aim for an early morning or late afternoon visit.

5. **Sagrada Família**: Pre-book your tickets online to skip the lines. Visit during off-peak hours or consider exploring the exterior if you're not interested in going inside.

6. **La Rambla:** While a famous street, it's often crowded. Try visiting early in the morning for a more relaxed experience.

7. **Restaurants**: Make reservations for popular restaurants in advance to ensure you get a table without waiting.

8. **Transport**: Use public transportation to avoid traffic and parking issues. The metro and buses are efficient ways to get around.

9. **Barri Gòtic:** This historic neighborhood can get crowded, but exploring its narrow streets early in the day can give you a more authentic experience.

10. **Beach Visits**: If you're interested in the beach, go early in the morning to secure a good spot before the crowds arrive.

11. **Local Markets:** Visit local markets like Mercat de la Boqueria early in the morning for a less chaotic shopping experience.

12. **Day Trips:** Consider taking day trips to nearby destinations like Montserrat, Girona, or the Costa Brava to escape the city crowds for a while.

13. **Museums:** Some museums offer free or discounted entry on specific days or during certain hours. Take

advantage of these times to explore cultural attractions without the peak crowds.

14. **Language**: Learning a few basic Spanish or Catalan phrases can help you navigate and interact with locals, enhancing your experience.

Have it at the back of your mind that the key is to plan ahead and be flexible. Barcelona has a lot to offer beyond the well-known attractions, so exploring off the beaten path can lead to some truly memorable experiences.

Chapter 10: Samples of Travel Itinerary

Barbados 3-Day Itinerary

Here's a 3-day travel itinerary for Barbados:

Day 1: Explore Bridgetown and Relax on the Beach

- Morning: Start your day with a visit to Bridgetown's historic sites, such as the Parliament Buildings and St. Michael's Cathedral.
- Afternoon: Head to Carlisle Bay for some

snorkeling and beach time. You can also visit the Barbados Museum & Historical Society.

- Evening: Enjoy a sunset dinner at a waterfront restaurant in Bridgetown, sampling local seafood and Caribbean cuisine.

Day 2: Discover the East Coast and Nature

- Morning: Drive to Bathsheba on the rugged east coast. Marvel at the dramatic rock formations and enjoy a walk on the picturesque beaches.
- Afternoon: Explore Hunte's Gardens, a lush tropical paradise with unique plants and pathways.
- Evening: Experience Oistins Fish Fry for a true Bajan culinary experience, featuring fresh seafood and lively music.

Day 3: Island Adventure and Culture

- Morning: Take a catamaran cruise to swim with sea turtles and snorkel in clear waters.

Many tours also include a delicious lunch onboard.

- Afternoon: Visit the historic plantation house and gardens of St. Nicholas Abbey. Learn about the island's sugar and rum history.
- Evening: Wrap up your trip with a lively Caribbean rum tasting and dinner at a local rum shop or beachside restaurant.

Remember, this is just a suggested itinerary. Barbados offers a wide range of activities and attractions, so feel free to tailor the plan to your preferences. Enjoy your trip.

5-Day Barbados Itinerary

Sure, here's a 5-day itinerary for your trip to Barbados:

Day 1: Arrival and Relaxation

- Arrive in Barbados and check in to your accommodation.
- Spend the afternoon at one of the beautiful beaches, such as Crane Beach or Miami Beach, to relax and unwind.

- In the evening, enjoy a local seafood dinner at a beachfront restaurant.

Day 2: Bridgetown and Cultural Exploration

- Visit Bridgetown, the capital city. Explore historic sites like St. Michael's Cathedral and Parliament Buildings.
- Take a walk along the boardwalk and enjoy the views of the coastline.
- Afternoon visit to the Barbados Museum to learn about the island's history and culture.
- Have dinner at a local Bajan restaurant to savor traditional dishes.

Day 3: Adventure and Nature

- Begin your day with an adventure at Harrison's Cave, a stunning underground limestone cave.
- Head to the east coast to visit Bathsheba, famous for its rugged beauty and surfing spots.
- Enjoy a scenic hike in the Barbados Wildlife Reserve, where you can

see green monkeys and other local wildlife.

- Wrap up the day with a relaxing sunset catamaran cruise along the coast.

Day 4: Beach Day and Water Activities

- Spend the morning at Carlisle Bay, known for its clear waters and snorkeling opportunities.
- Try your hand at water sports like jet skiing, paddleboarding, or kayaking.
- Afternoon visit to the Mount Gay Rum Distillery for a tour and tasting session.
- Enjoy a lively evening at the Oistins Fish Fry, a local gathering with food, music, and dancing.

Day 5: Nature and Farewell

- Start your day with a visit to the Flower Forest, a botanical garden showcasing exotic plants.
- Explore the Andromeda Botanic Gardens with its lush landscapes and ocean views.

- Relax at the beach, take a swim, or do some last-minute shopping for souvenirs.
- Wrap up your trip with a farewell dinner at a fine dining restaurant, enjoying the flavors of Barbadian cuisine.

Remember that this itinerary can be adjusted based on your interests and preferences. Enjoy your trip to Barbados.

7-Day Barbados Itinerary

Here's a 7-day itinerary for your trip to Barbados:

Day 1: Arrival and Beach Time

- Arrive in Barbados and check in to your accommodation.
- Spend the afternoon relaxing on the beautiful beaches of the West Coast, such as Mullins Beach or Paynes Bay.
- Enjoy a seafood dinner at a beachfront restaurant.

Day 2: Bridgetown Exploration

- Explore Bridgetown, the capital city.
- Visit the historic Garrison area, a UNESCO World Heritage site.

- Tour the Barbados Museum to learn about the island's history and culture.
- Enjoy lunch at a local eatery.
- Afternoon visit to Carlisle Bay for snorkeling or a catamaran cruise.

Day 3: East Coast Adventure

- Drive to the rugged East Coast for a change of scenery.
- Hike in Bathsheba and take in the stunning coastal views.
- Visit the Andromeda Botanic Gardens.
- Lunch at a local restaurant.
- Relax on one of the more secluded East Coast beaches.

Day 4: Oistins and Nightlife

- Head to Oistins Fish Fry for a lively local dinner and entertainment.
- Try the freshly caught fish and other Bajan dishes.
- Stay for the music and dancing.

Day 5: Island Tour

- Take a guided island tour to explore attractions like

Harrison's Cave and Welchman Hall Gully.

- Visit St. Nicholas Abbey, a historic plantation house and rum distillery.
- Enjoy a rum tasting and lunch on the estate.

Day 6: Water Sports and Sunset

- Spend the morning engaging in water sports like jet skiing, paddleboarding, or kite surfing.
- Afternoon visit to Animal Flower Cave.
- Enjoy a sunset cocktail cruise along the coast.

Day 7: Relaxation and Farewell

- Spend your last day enjoying a spa treatment or leisurely beach time.
- Shop for souvenirs and local crafts.
- Dine at an upscale restaurant for a final memorable meal.

Know that this is just a suggested itinerary and can be adjusted based on your interests and preferences. Have a great trip to Barbados.

10-Day Barbados Itinerary

A suggested 10-day itinerary for your trip to Barbados:

Day 1: Arrival

- Arrive in Barbados and settle into your accommodation.
- Relax on one of the beautiful beaches, like Crane Beach or Miami Beach.
- Enjoy a traditional Bajan dinner at a local restaurant.

Day 2: Bridgetown and History

- Explore Bridgetown, the capital city, visiting sites like Parliament Buildings and Independence Square.
- Visit the Barbados Museum and Historical Society to learn about the island's history.
- Enjoy a sunset catamaran cruise along the coastline.

Day 3: Adventure and Nature

- Take a day trip to Harrison's Cave, an impressive underground cave system.
- Enjoy outdoor activities like zip-lining, hiking, or exploring the Animal Flower Cave.

- Relax at a beachside bar and try some local cocktails.

Day 4: East Coast Exploration
- Drive along the scenic East Coast, stopping at Bathsheba to admire the rugged coastline.
- Visit the Andromeda Botanic Gardens for a serene nature walk.
- Experience local cuisine at a beachfront restaurant.

Day 5: Wildlife and Marine Life
- Explore the Barbados Wildlife Reserve to see animals like green monkeys.
- Snorkel or scuba dive to explore the vibrant marine life in Carlisle Bay.
- Try flying fish, a Bajan delicacy, for lunch.

Day 6: Rum and Culinary Delights
- Take a tour of the Mount Gay Rum Distillery and learn about the island's rum-making history.
- Enjoy a Bajan cooking class to learn how to prepare local dishes.

- Attend a lively dinner show featuring traditional Bajan music and dance.

Day 7: Beach Day
- Spend a full day relaxing on one of Barbados' stunning beaches.
- Try water sports like surfing, paddleboarding, or jet skiing.
- Treat yourself to a beachfront massage or spa treatment.

Day 8: Plantation and Gardens
- Visit St. Nicholas Abbey, a historic plantation house, and rum distillery.
- Explore the nearby Hunte's Gardens, a lush and tropical oasis.
- Enjoy a sunset dinner at a seaside restaurant.

Day 9: Cultural Immersion
- Participate in a local arts and crafts workshop.
- Visit the Arlington House Museum to learn about the island's culture and heritage.
- Explore Oistins Fish Fry for a taste of local street food and live music.

Day 10: Departure

- Spend your last morning souvenir shopping or relaxing on the beach.
- Check out of your accommodation and head to the airport for your departure.

Always customize the itinerary based on your preferences and any special events or attractions happening during your visit. Enjoy your trip to Barbados.

Printed in Great Britain
by Amazon

27708512R00059